Animal Gallery

For Simon

OXFORD
UNIVERSITY PRESS

Great Clarendon Street, Oxford OX2 6DP

Oxford University Press is a department of the University of Oxford.
It furthers the University's objective of excellence in research, scholarship,
and education by publishing worldwide in

Oxford   New York

Auckland   Cape Town   Dar es Salaam   Hong Kong   Karachi
Kuala Lumpur   Madrid   Melbourne   Mexico City   Nairobi
New Delhi   Shanghai   Taipei   Toronto

With offices in
Argentina   Austria   Brazil   Chile   Czech Republic   France   Greece
Guatemala   Hungary   Italy   Japan   Poland   Portugal   Singapore
South Korea   Switzerland   Thailand   Turkey   Ukraine   Vietnam

Oxford is a registered trade mark of Oxford University Press
in the UK and in certain other countries

© Brian Wildsmith 1967, 1968, 2008

The moral rights of the author/illustrator have been asserted
Database right Oxford University Press (maker)

Wild Animals first published 1967, *Fishes* first published 1968,
Birds first published 1967
Brian Wildsmith's Animal Gallery first published 2008
First published in paperback in 2010

British Library Cataloguing in Publication Data:
Data available

ISBN: 978-0-19-272794-7 (paperback)

10 9 8 7 6 5 4 3 2 1

Printed in China

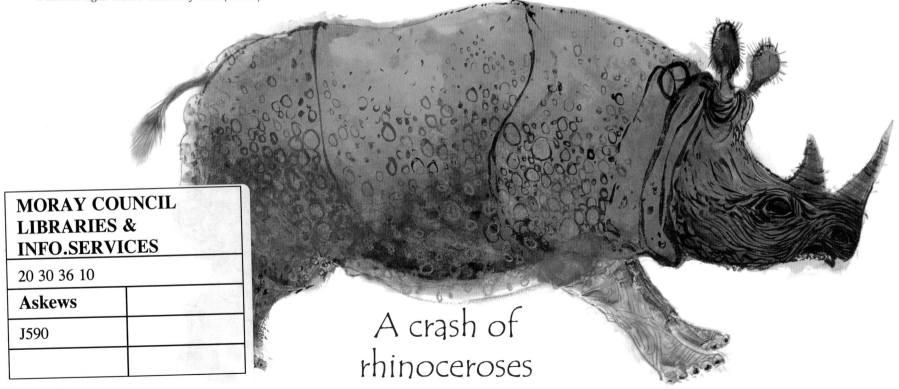

A crash of
rhinoceroses

Brian Wildsmith's Animal Gallery

OXFORD

UNIVERSITY PRESS

A pride of lions

A herd
of sea horses

A corps
of giraffes

A wedge
of swans

A skulk
of foxes

A herd of hippopotami

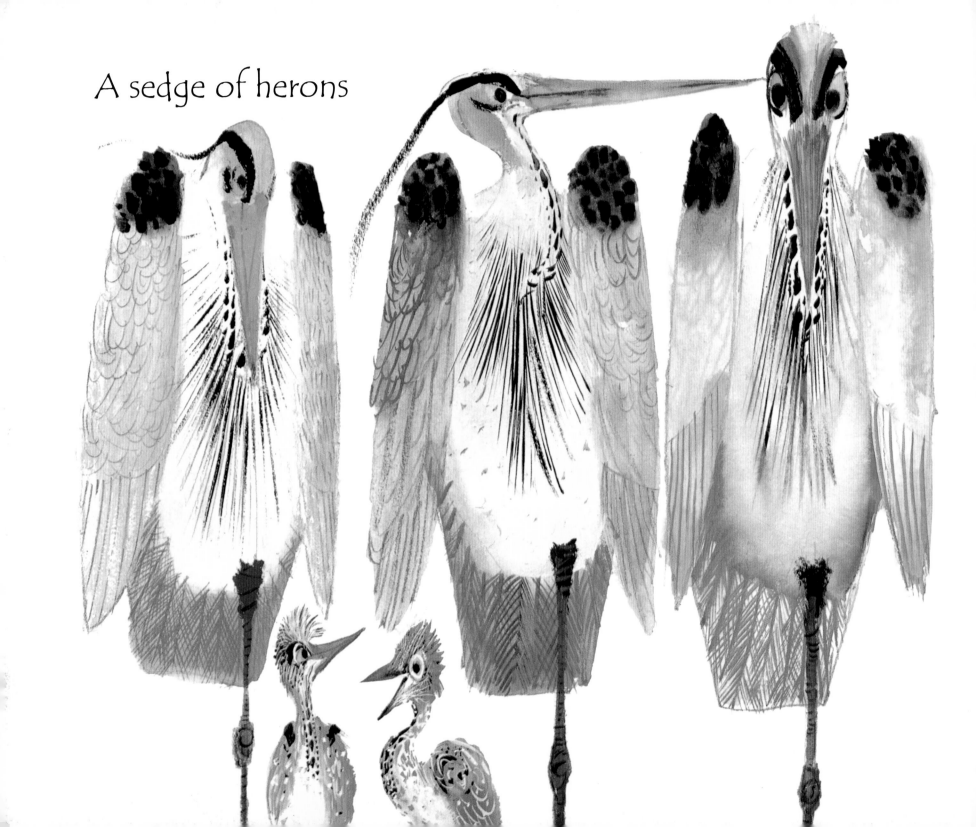

A sedge of herons

A flotilla
of swordfish

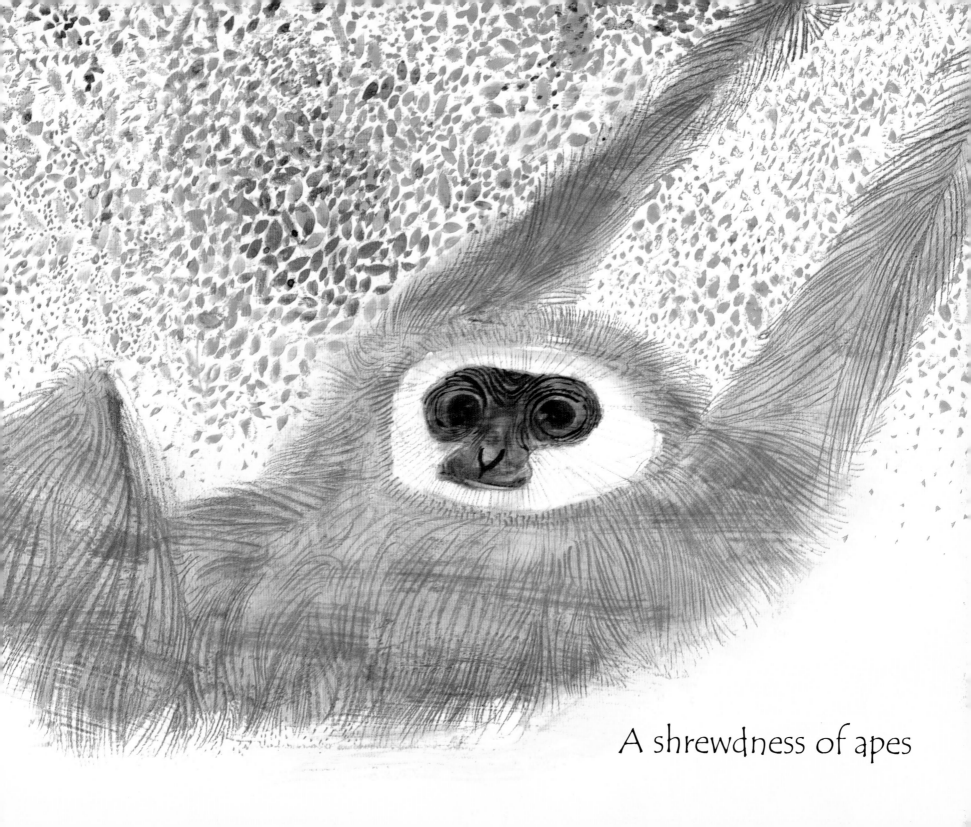

A shrewdness of apes

A troop of kangaroos

A party of rainbow fish

An ambush
of tigers

A glide of flying fish

A sloth of bears

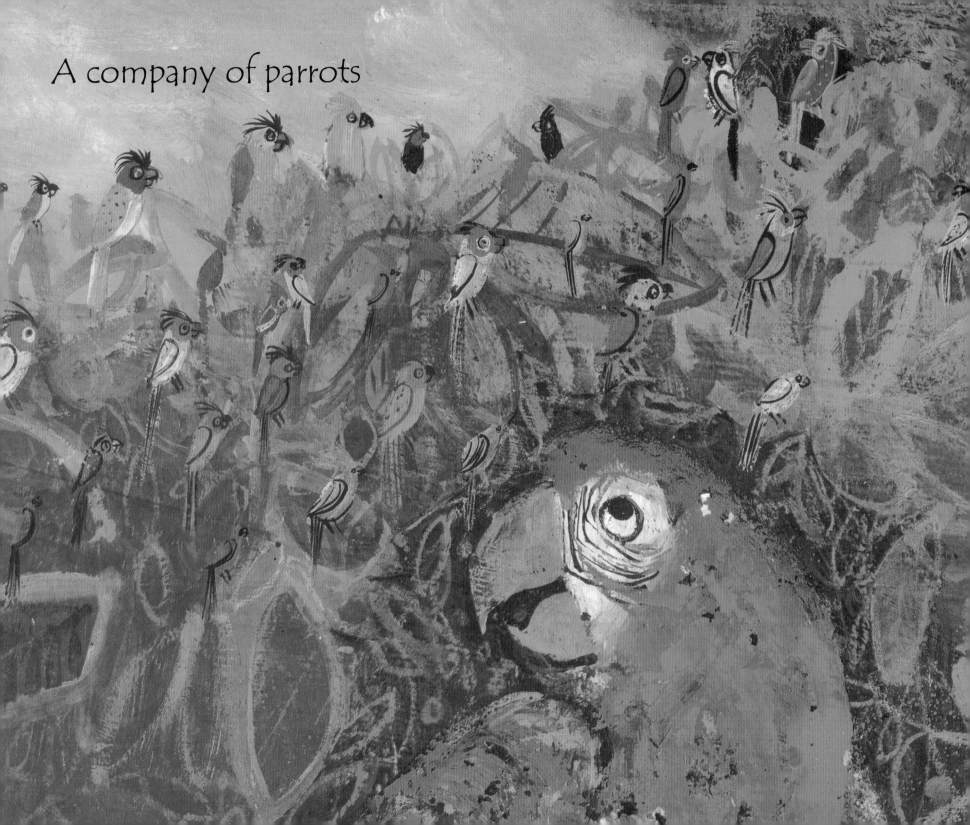

A company of parrots

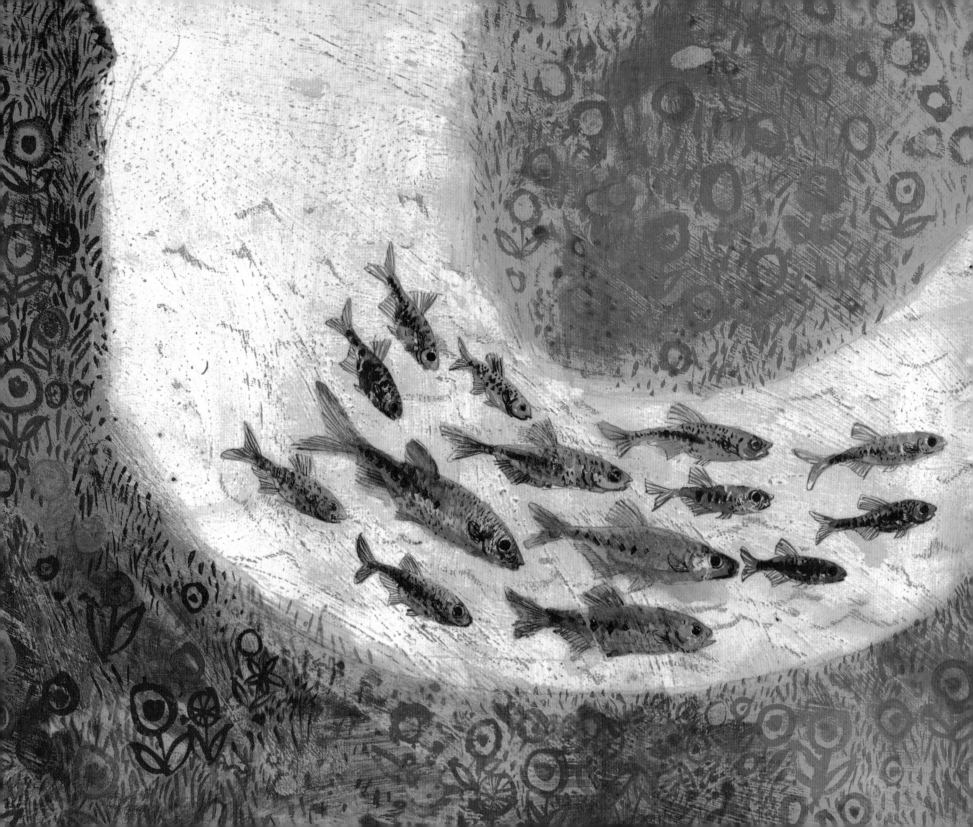

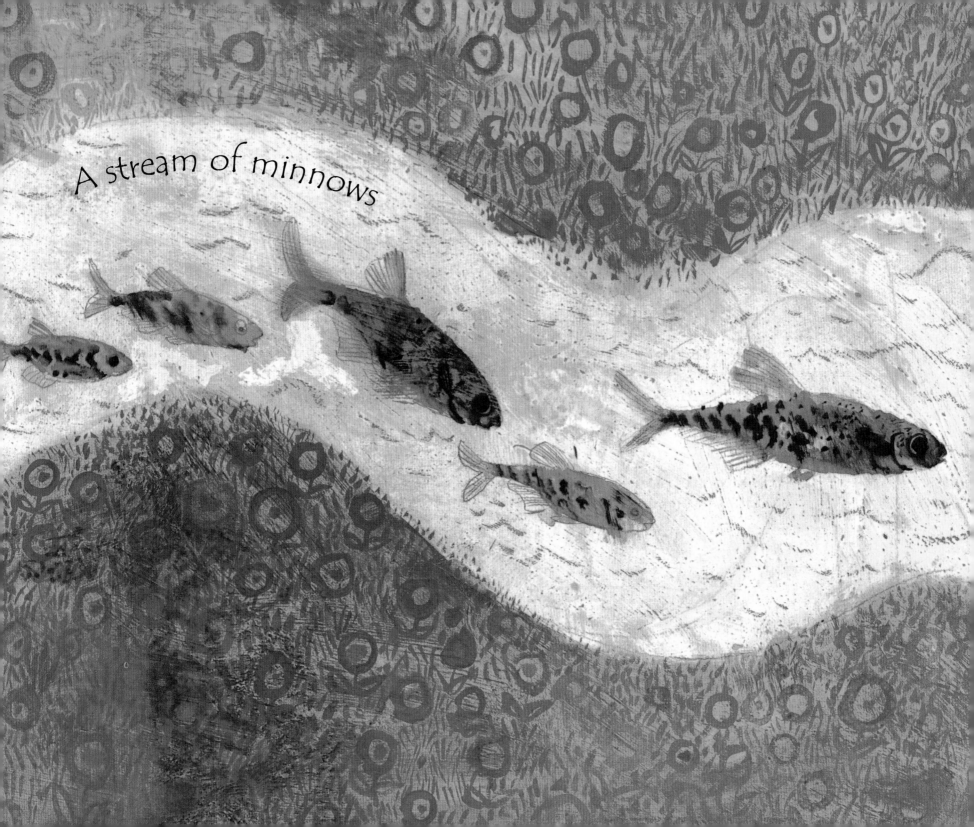

A stream of minnows

A stare of owls

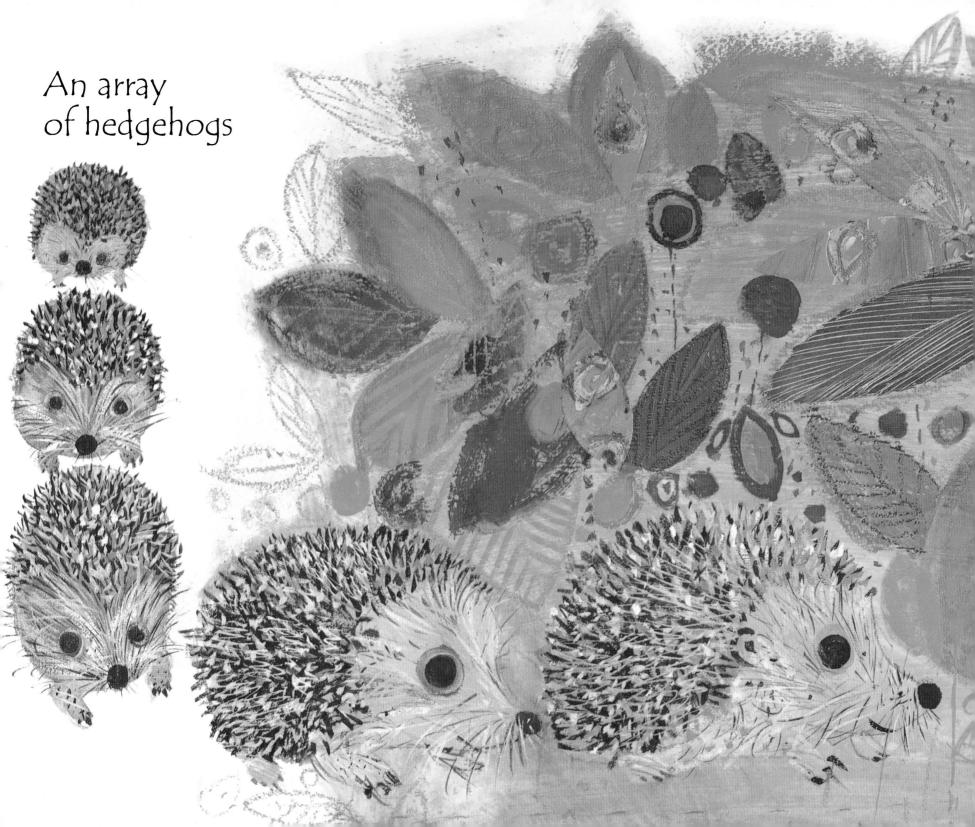

An array
of hedgehogs

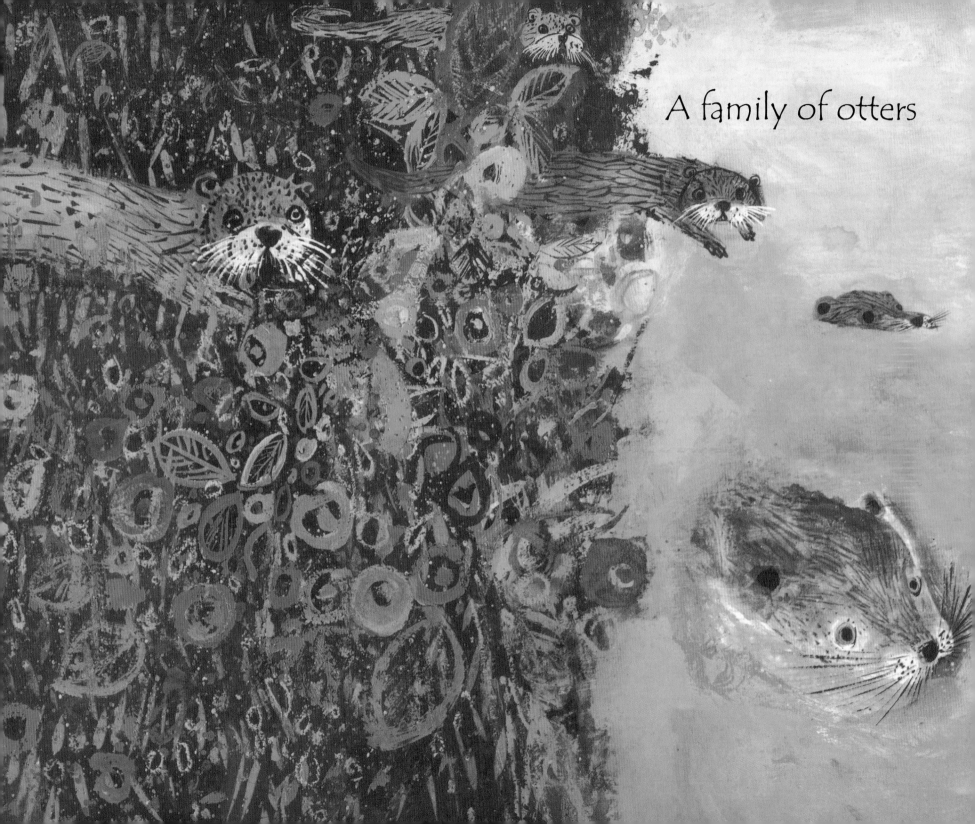

A family of otters

A hover of trout

A colony of penguins

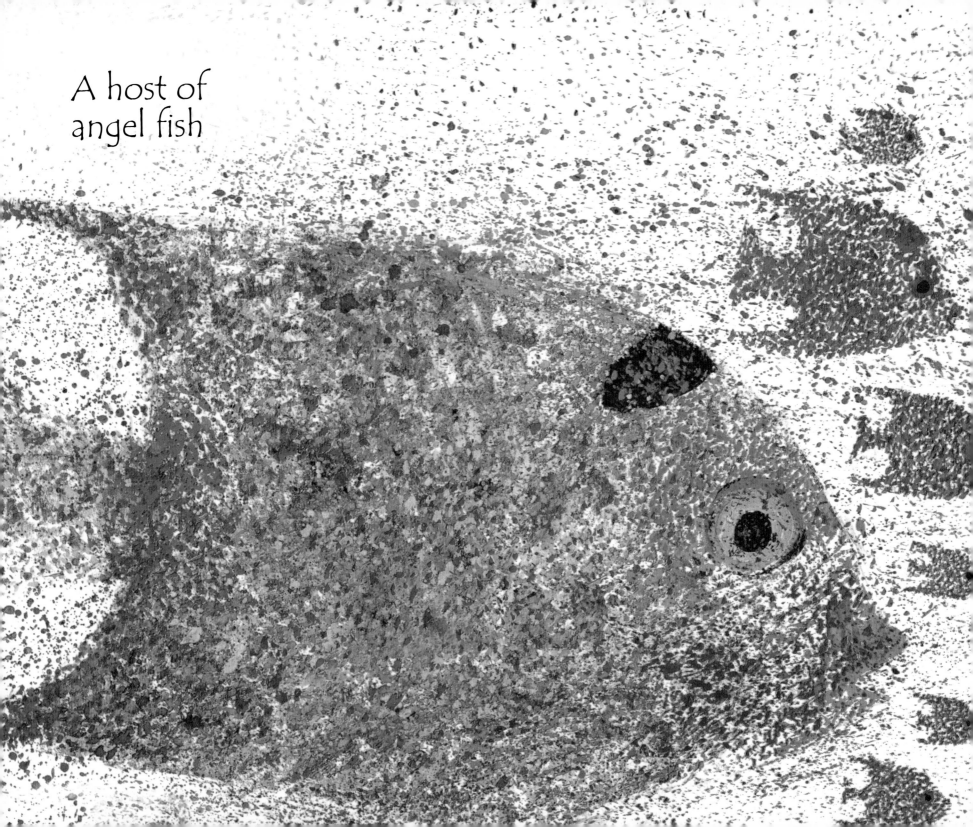

A host of
angel fish

A herd of reindeer

A nursery
of racoons

A rafter of turkeys

A lepe of leopards

A herd of elephants

A lodge
of beavers

A dray
of squirrels